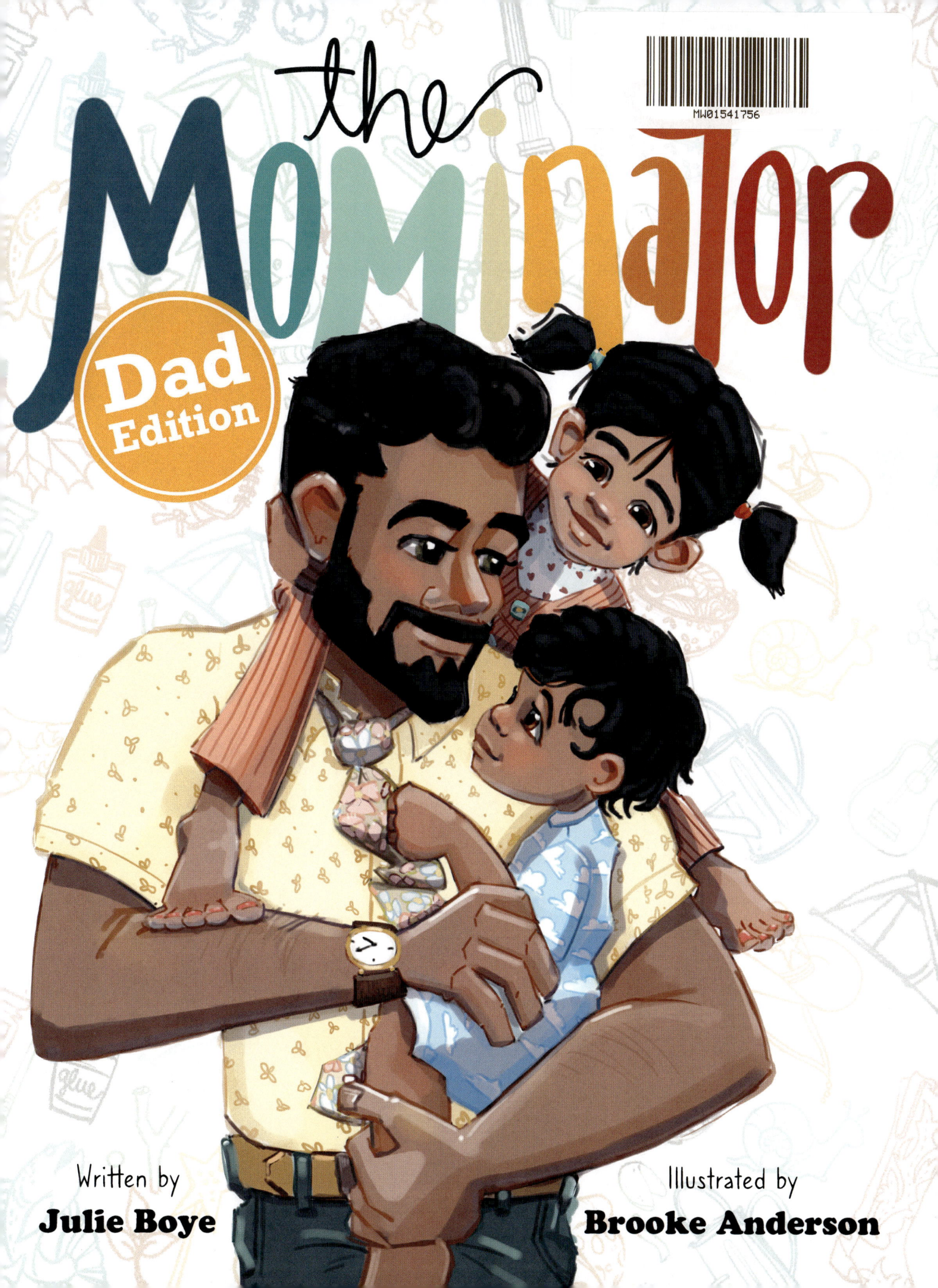

Text © 2022 Julie Boye

Illustrations © 2022 Brooke Anderson

All rights reserved.

No part of this book may be reproduced in any form whatsoever, whether by graphic, visual, electronic, film, microfilm, tape recording, or any other means, without permission of the publisher, except in the case of brief passages embodied in critical reviews and articles.

ISBN-13: 978-1-7338465-3-0 (paperback)

978-1-7338465-4-7 (hardback)

978-1-7338465-5-4 (e-book)

Published by The Boye Family Jewels

Cover design by Brooke Anderson

Typeset and interior design by Chelsea Jackson

Edited by Chelsea Jackson, Jackson Writing and Editing, LLC

To my dad, Jon, and husband, Alex, the greatest dads and heroes to their kids! To all the mominators who make them look good. To my mini mominators—Adanna, India, Kenia, and Nayoma. And special mention to the daddies in the making—Zander, Ari, Treyu, and Niko.

Julie

To learn more about Julie, visit theboyefamilyjewels.com or @theboyefamilyjewels on Instagram and YouTube.

To my dad, who has always been my biggest fan; my husband Dustin; and our boys, Emmett, Adler, and Riggs. I love you all!

Brooke

To learn more about Brooke, visit @brookeknightillu on Instagram.

Sometimes when you're

little, you get in the

middle

and prevent Dad from

getting things **done**.

You just want to **play**,

but you get in the way

when Dad's **working**,

and that ain't no **fun**!

There's so much to **learn** like waiting your **turn** and pushing Mom's buttons just **right**.

With much on her **plate**, it's hard to **relate** when Mom wants to throw in the **towel**.

'Cuz even one **child** can be super **wild**, but oh how she tries not to **scowl**.

There's one **special** guy who's Mom's best **ally**. His **name** has many a-meaning.

He jumps and he **flies**,

Spiderman in **disguise**!

He's a **hero** with Mom's intervening.

A **professional** chef—and

a little tone-**deaf**—but

he **dances** and that's just the start.

At the end of the **day**,

he picks you up from **ballet**

and **greets** Mom after being apart.

Life constantly **changes** and Dad **rearranges** a day that becomes u n e x p e c t e d.

On the days that you **lose**, he's been in your **shoes** when you're angry and feeling **rejected**.

Get back in the **saddle**.

He'll help fight your **battle**

'cuz dads don't give up, nor should **you**.

He's one of a **kind**,
and when homework's **assigned**,
he steps in to **help** when it's due.

He's the best **bodyguard**, and he **tries** really hard, even though he makes quite a big **mess**.

The **memories** stay

when you work hard at **play**

'cuz Dad often responds with a "**Yes**!"

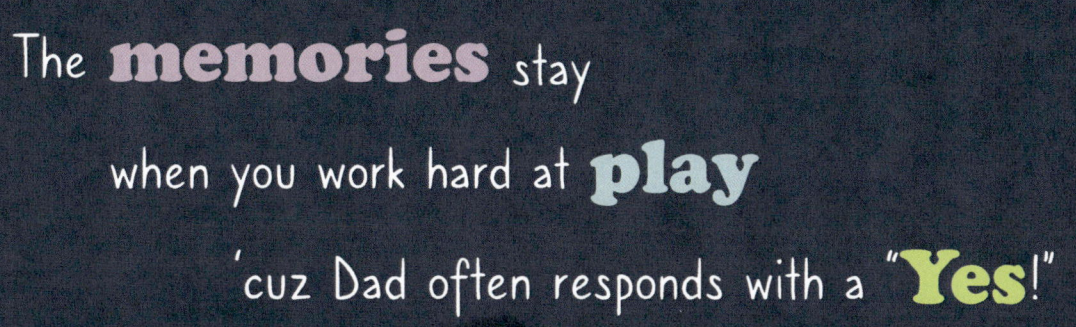

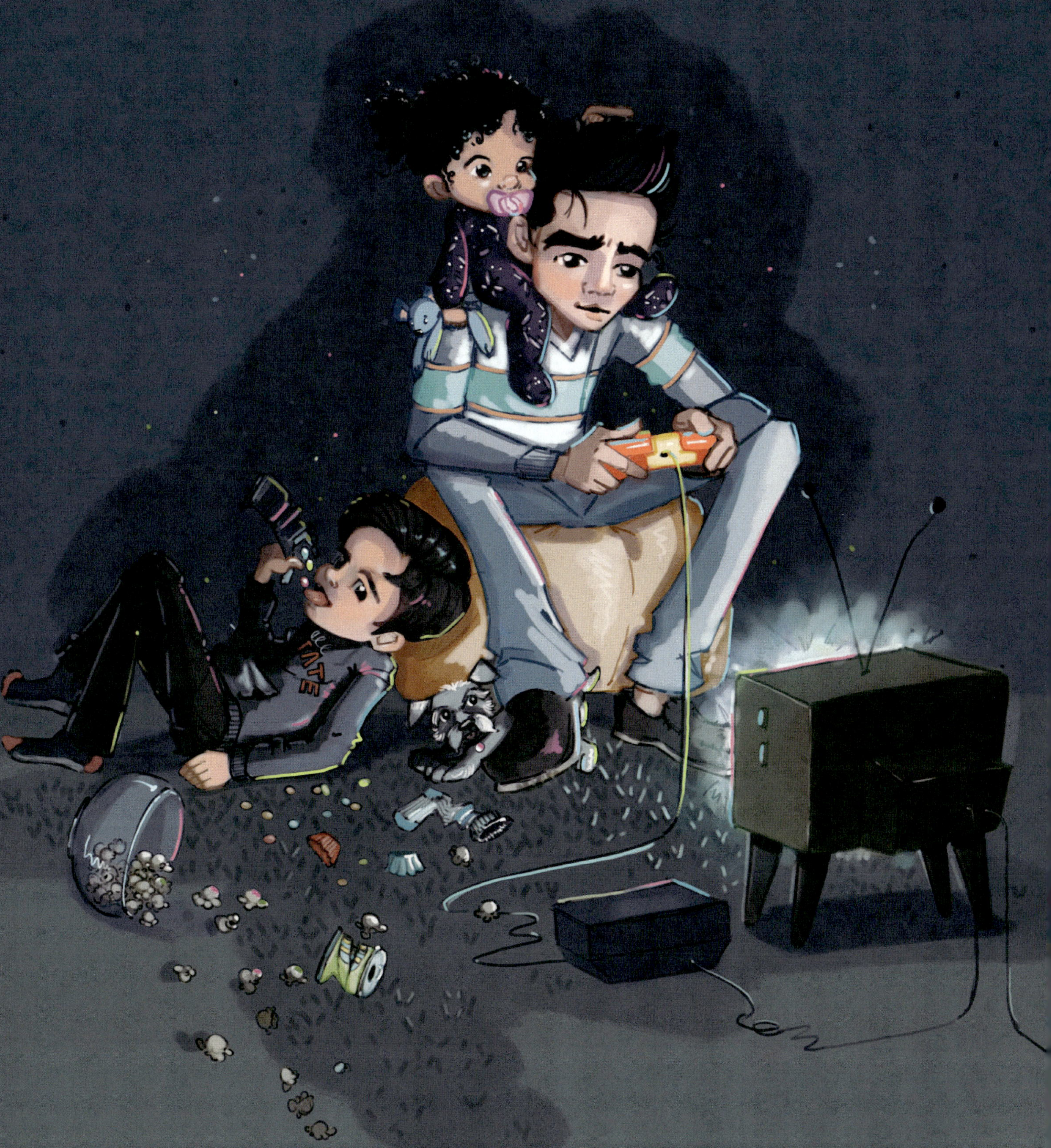

If you show that you're **brave**,
 he'll teach you to **shave**
  'cuz dads can be really great **teachers**.

He's your #1 **fan** when you become a **man**, especially up in the **bleachers**.

And on your **birthdate**

when you're finally eight

with **Jesus** you'll make a big **promise**.

Along with your **dad**,
He's your greatest **comrade**.
Of Him you'll always bear **witness**.

Dad will **miss** a work meeting to get some good seating. He **loves** to sit next to his **wife**.

'Cuz when you **succeed**

he's **supportive** indeed,

even though he now **fears** for his life!

When Dad mows the lawn, you try to catch on.
It's a **challenge** when you're only four!
He'll **show** you the way but might go
astray when he sees a bad call and the score.

He'll try not to **cry**,
it feels like goodbye,
when he gives you away—you're all **grown**!

And if your **circumstance**

never gave you the chance

to meet him or talk face to face,

remember this **truth**

while you're in your youth,

hold it dear to your **heart** just in case:

Your dad here on **earth** who's part of your **birth** gets help when he cannot come **through**.

Julie Boye

is still the O.G. Mominator with eight kids—four girls and four boys. So she gets it. Her family has been featured on Dr. Oz, Daily Mail Online in the UK, the British talk show "Loose Women," and several other TV networks and podcasts. She is an opinion columnist for the Deseret News, a fitness enthusiast, and considers herself a foodie. She enjoys alone time. Lots of alone time! She also loves watching her kids excel in their activities and her husband kill it on stage!

Brooke Anderson

is a mom of three young energetic boys. She began art classes at age nine after begging her mom for a year. She studied traditional art under several local artists in Utah. She made the switch to digital and found her niche for illustration, which was a better fit while juggling mommy life. Aside from drawing and mom stuff, she likes to play pickleball and soccer, listen to Indie folk music, go on walks, and read to her boys. Oh and she loves to devour almond butter!

Enjoy the book?
Leave a review on Amazon and share it with your friends!

Check out Julie's first book! Available on Amazon!

Meet the world's greatest heroines—**Mominators**! They may be covered in baby drool, cheering on the sidelines at the top of their lungs, or blubbering messes over the first day of school, but moms have superpowers. And yet they still kneel to pray for a divine helping hand when days get to be too much.

Made in the USA
Las Vegas, NV
25 April 2022